BIBLE MEMORY VERSE GAMES FOR CHILDREN

Therefore everyone who hears
these words of mine and
puts them into practice
is like a wise man who
built his house on the rock.
—Matt. 7:24

BIBLE MEMORY VERSE GAMES FOR CHILDREN

50 Fun and Creative Activities to Help Kids Learn—and Remember—God's Word

DON AND KATHLEEN MILLER

Beacon Hill Press of Kansas City
Kansas City, Missouri

Copyright 1995

by Beacon Hill Press of Kansas City

ISBN 083-411-5395

Printed in the
United States of America

Cover design: Ted Ferguson

10   9   8   7   6   5   4   3   2

To our son Luke—
who enjoys memorizing God's Word

CONTENTS

INTRODUCTION

The purpose of teaching children to memorize Bible verses is found in Ps. 119:11: "I have hidden your word in my heart that I might not sin against you." Each Bible lesson taught to children needs to include a Scripture verse for them to memorize. The Scripture verse should reinforce the lesson. The memory verse methods in this book provide opportunities for children to see and hear the verse repeatedly. Repetition is very important.

There are two sections included. Section 1 contains methods to introduce memory verses. Section 2 contains methods to help children master memory verses. Most of the methods are games or contests that make memorizing Bible verses fun and exciting.

Methods to Introduce Memory Verses

Balloon Bust

Materials:
1. Balloons 6" to 9" in diameter, one balloon for each word in the memory verse
2. Thumbtacks
3. Plywood or bulletin board, 4' x 4'
4. Three throwing darts
5. Black marker
6. Chair
7. Masking tape

Preparation:
1. Inflate the balloons.
2. Write each word of the memory verse on a separate balloon with the black marker.
3. Use thumbtacks to attach the lip of each balloon to the plywood or bulletin board. Place the balloons in the correct order so the children can read the memory verse.
4. Place three or four tape lines about 6" apart on the floor in front of the board, designating the distance for players of different ages.

Game Rules:
1. Divide the children into two teams: Team A and Team B (for example, a boys' team and a girls' team).
2. Direct the children to say the memory verse two or three times.
3. Choose a child from Team A to stand behind the appropriate tape line.
4. The child has three chances to pop one of the balloons with the darts.
5. Award team points for each balloon the child pops. Award bonus points if the child can say the memory verse.
6. Choose a child from Team B to stand behind one of the lines. Proceed through steps 4 and 5.
7. Continue playing the game until all the balloons have been popped.
8. The team with the most points wins.

Balloon Line

Materials:
1. One clothespin for each word in the memory verse
2. One balloon for each word in the memory verse
3. 25' of ¼" rope
4. Black marker

Preparation:
1. Inflate the balloons.
2. Write each word of the memory verse on a separate balloon.
3. Use clothespins to attach the balloons to the rope. Place the balloons in the correct order so the children can read the memory verse.

Game Rules:
1. Select two children to come to the front of the classroom and hold the rope.
2. Divide the children into two teams: Team A and Team B (for example, a boys' team and a girls' team).
3. Choose a child from Team A to stand and say the memory verse.
4. Award team points if the child says the verse correctly.
5. Pop one of the balloons.
6. Choose a child from Team B to stand and say the memory verse. Proceed through steps 4 and 5.
7. Continue playing the game until you have popped all the balloons and the children are saying the verse by memory.
8. The team with the most points wins.

14

Baseball Throw

Materials:

1. Three rubber balls or Nerf balls
2. Poster board
3. Black marker
4. Masking tape

Preparation:

1. From the poster board, cut cards approximately 4" x 19". Cut as many cards as there are words in the memory verse.
2. Fold the cards in half so they stand like tepees.
3. Write each word of the memory verse on a card.
4. Place the cards in sequential order across the front of the classroom.
5. Place the balls at the front of the classroom.
6. Place three or four tape lines about 6" apart on the floor, designating the distance for players of different ages.

Game Rules:

1. Divide the children into two teams: Team A and Team B (for example, a boys' team and a girls' team).
2. Direct the children to say the memory verse two or three times.
3. Choose a child from Team A to come to the front of the classroom and say the memory verse.
4. Give the child a ball. The child has three chances to knock over a card.
5. Award the child a prize or team points if he or she knocks over a card.
6. Award the child's team points if he or she says the verse correctly.
7. Choose a child from Team B to come to the front of the classroom. Proceed through steps 4, 5, and 6. Increase the number of team points you award each time, since there are fewer words standing and the verse becomes harder to say.
8. Continue playing the game until all the cards are knocked down.
9. The team with the most points wins.

Beanbag Toss

Materials:
1. Three beanbags
2. Poster board
3. Black marker
4. Masking tape

Preparation:
1. From the poster board, cut cards approximately 6" x 16". Cut as many cards as there are words in the memory verse.
2. Fold the cards in half and stand them like tepees.
3. Write each word of the memory verse on a card.
4. Place the cards in sequential order across the front of the classroom.
5. Place the beanbags at the front of the classroom.
6. Place three or four tape lines about 6" apart on the floor, designating the distance for players of different ages.

Game Rules:
1. Divide the children into two teams: Team A and Team B (for example, a boys' team and a girls' team).
2. Direct the children to say the memory verse two or three times.
3. Select a child from Team A to come to the front of the classroom and say the memory verse.
4. Give the child three beanbags, one for each chance to knock over a card.
5. Award the child a prize or team points if he or she knocks over a card.
6. Award the child's team points if he or she says the verse correctly.
7. Choose a child from Team B to come to the front of the classroom. Proceed through steps 4, 5, and 6. Increase the number of team points you award each time, since there are fewer words standing and the verse becomes harder to say.
8. Continue playing the game until all the words are knocked over.
9. The team with the most points wins.

Bread of Life

Materials:

1. Poster board
2. Bulletin board
3. Thumbtacks
4. Loaf of bread
5. Black and brown markers
6. Table

Preparation:

1. From the poster board, cut cards the shape and size of bread slices. Cut as many cards as there are words in the memory verse.
2. Write each word of the memory verse on a card. Outline the cards in brown to look like bread crust.
3. Take the loaf of bread out of the plastic bag, and place a card between each slice.
4. Put the bread back into the plastic bag.
5. Place the loaf of bread onto the table at the front of the classroom.

Game Rules:

1. Tell the children that Jesus described himself as the "bread of life" (John 6:35).
2. Take the loaf of bread out of the plastic bag.
3. Pull out three or four slices of bread, and explain how the Word of God is food for their spirit.
4. Take the cards out of the bread, and tack them in correct order onto the bulletin board.
5. Divide the children into two teams: Team A and Team B (for example, a boys' team and a girls' team).
6. Choose a child from Team A to come to the front of the classroom and read the memory verse on the bulletin board.
7. Remove a bread-slice card from the bulletin board, and ask the child to say the verse.
8. Award the child a prize or team points if he or she can say the verse correctly.
9. Choose a child from Team B to come to the front of the classroom and say the memory verse. Proceed through steps 7 and 8.
10. Continue playing the game until all the bread-slice cards have been removed from the bulletin board.
11. The team with the most points wins.

Card Line

Materials:
1. 25' of ¼" rope
2. Clothespins
3. Poster board
4. Black marker

Preparation:
1. From the poster board, cut cards approximately 5" x 10". Cut as many cards as there are words in the memory verse.
2. Write each word of the memory verse on a separate card.
3. Use clothespins to attach the cards to the rope in sequential order.

Game Rules:
1. Select two children to come to the front of the classroom and hold the rope.
2. Divide the children into teams: Team A and Team B (for example, a boys' team and a girls' team).
3. Choose a child from Team A to stand and say the memory verse.
4. Award team points if the child says the verse correctly.
5. Remove one card from the rope.
6. Choose a child from Team B to come to the front of the classroom and say the memory verse. Proceed through steps 4 and 5.
7. Continue playing the game until you have removed all the cards and the children are saying the verse by memory.
8. The team with the most points wins.

Disappearing Words

Materials:
1. Marker board
2. Markers for the marker board
3. Eraser

Preparation:
1. Write the memory verse on the marker board.

Game Rules:
1. Divide the children into two teams: Team A and Team B (for example, a boys' team and a girls' team).
2. Choose a child from Team A to stand and say the memory verse.
3. Award team points if the child says the verse correctly.
4. Erase one word from the marker board.
5. Choose a child from Team B to stand and say the memory verse. Proceed through steps 3 and 4.
6. Continue playing until you have erased all the words and the children are saying the verse by memory.
7. The team with the most points wins.

Goin' Fishin'

Materials:

1. 25' of ¼" rope
2. Clothespins
3. Yellow poster board
4. Black marker

Preparation:

1. Use the poster board to cut out fish shapes. Cut out as many fish as there are words in the memory verse.
2. Write each word of the memory verse on a fish.
3. Use clothespins to attach the fish to the rope in sequential order.

Game Rules:

1. Tell the boys and girls that they can catch something good from the Word of God.
2. Select two children to come to the front of the classroom and hold the stringer of fish.
3. Divide the children into two teams: Team A and Team B (for example, a boys' team and a girls' team).
4. Choose a child from Team A to stand and say the memory verse.
5. Award team points if the child says the verse correctly.
6. Remove one fish from the stringer.
7. Choose a child from Team B to stand and say the memory verse. Proceed through steps 5 and 6.
8. Award team points if the child says the verse correctly.
9. Continue playing the game until you have removed all the fish and the children are saying the verse by memory.
10. The team with the most points wins.

Gospel Power

Materials:
1. 5" x 8" index cards
2. Black marker
3. Rubber bands
4. Rubber band gun (or a clothespin and a stick)
5. Table large enough to place memory verse cards across it
6. Masking tape

Preparation:
1. Write each word of the memory verse on a separate index card.
2. Place the cards in sequential order on the table, standing them up by using another card perpendicular behind each one.
3. Place three or four tape lines about 6" apart on the floor, designating the distance for players of different ages.

Game Rules:
1. Divide the children into two teams: Team A and Team B (for example, a boys' team and a girls' team).
2. Select a child from Team A to come to the front of the class.
3. Give the child a rubber band gun and three rubber bands, one for each chance to shoot down a word card.
4. Award a prize or team points for each word card the child knocks down.
5. Award a prize or team points if the child can say the memory verse correctly.
6. Select a child from Team B to come to the front of the classroom. Proceed through steps 3, 4, and 5.
7. Continue playing the game until there are no memory verse word cards standing and the children are saying the verse by memory.
8. The team with the most points wins.

Grid Game

Materials:
1. Chalkboard or marker board
2. Poster board
3. Masking tape
4. Black marker
5. Chalk for chalkboard or dry erase markers for marker board
6. Yard stick or straight edge

Preparation:
1. Use the poster board to cut cards, 6" by 8". Cut twice as many cards as there are words in the memory verse.
2. Write each word of the memory verse on a card, and write a number on each card in sequential order (1, 2, 3, and so on).
3. Make a set of cards for each team.
4. Use the chalkboard or marker board to create two grids. Make each grid by drawing vertical and horizontal lines on the chalkboard or marker board. Lines need to be drawn so the cards (6" by 8") fit inside the spaces of the grid. Number each space 1, 2, 3, and so on.

Game Rules:
1. Divide the children into two teams: Team A and Team B (e.g., a boy's team and a girl's team).
2. Select a pair of children from Team A and a pair of children from Team B to come to the front of the classroom. The two pairs of children should be of similar age or ability. Give each pair a set of cards.
3. On the count of three, direct the children to tape the memory verse cards in the correct order on the grid. Tell the children to use the numbers on the back to help them place the cards in order.
4. The first pair of children to place the memory verse cards in correct order and read the verse wins.
5. Award prize or points to the team the pair of children represent. (A or B)
6. Select another pair of children from each team to come to the front of the classroom. Proceed through steps three, four, and five.
7. Continue playing the game for several rounds.
8. The team with the most points wins.

Alternative Idea:
1. If a large chalkboard or marker board is unavailable, use two large sheets of white paper (at least 3' wide by 6' long) to create each grid.
2. Tape each grid to the front wall of the classroom.

Helpful Hint:
1. Create two tape sheets by tearing off piece of masking tape, rolling in small circles, and attaching to a card.
2. Give each team a tape sheet. Tell children to use the tape to attach cards to the grid.
3. Tape sheets allow the game to flow smoothly because there is less time spent tearing off pieces of tape.

Heavenly Mail

Materials:
1. Envelopes, 4⅛" by 9½" (business size), one for each word in the memory verse.
2. Poster board
3. Mailbag
4. Hat and attire for person delivering mail
5. Black marker

Preparation:
1. Use poster board to make cards 4" by 9". Cut one for each word of the memory verse.
2. Write each word of the memory verse on a card.
3. Place the cards in correct order. On the back of each card, place the number of the word as it appears in the verse. For example, on the back of the first word of the memory verse, write 1. On the back of the second word in the verse, write 2.
4. Place each card in an envelope and seal it.
5. Address the envelopes to individual children in class.
6. Put the addressed envelopes in the mailbag.
7. Select and dress an adult to deliver the mail.

Game Rules:
1. Mail person enters the classroom announcing, "Special delivery! I have a special delivery for the children in this class. I have a letter for _____ . (Mail person calls names of children who have envelopes addressed to them.)
2. Children open their envelopes.
3. Direct the children who received mail to come to the front of the classroom with the card they received in their envelope. Tell them to position themselves according to the number on the back of the card.
4. Children at the front of the classroom hold their cards for the other children to see.
5. Choose a child in the class who is not standing up front to read the memory verse. Then choose another child to read it. Have the memory verse read several times.
6. Direct one or two children who are holding cards to sit down. Choose another child to read the verse. Then select another child to read it.
7. Continue playing until all the children have sat down and the class can recite the memory verse.
8. Prize may be awarded to each child who reads or recites the memory verse.

Letter Scramble

Materials:
1. Marker board
2. Black marker for the marker board

Preparation:
1. Write the memory verse on the marker board by scrambling the letters of each word.
2. Leave enough space between the lines of scrambled words to write the correct words later.

Game Rules:
1. Divide the children into two teams: Team A and Team B (for example, a boys' team and a girls' team).
2. Choose a child from Team A to come to the front of the classroom and unscramble one word of the memory verse.
3. As the child spells the word correctly, write it above the scrambled word.
4. Award points to the team according to the number of letters in the word. For example, a three-letter word may be worth 300 points, a seven-letter word may be worth 700 points, and so on.
5. Choose a child from Team B to come to the front of the classroom. Proceed through steps 3 and 4.
6. Continue playing the game until the children have decoded each word of the memory verse.
7. Have the children say the memory verse.
8. The team with the most points wins.

Memory Character

Materials:

1. A character in costume (for example, any Bible character or "Faith Man")
2. Marker board
3. Markers for the marker board

Preparation:

1. Write the memory verse on the marker board.
2. Have the character in costume practice what he or she will say and do. For example, if Faith Man is visiting, he might say, "Boys and girls, I want you to know what makes me strong. It is the Word of God."
3. The character reads the memory verse on the board and then directs the children to say the memory verse several times.

Alternative Idea:

1. Invite a character to your class who does not know the memory verse. For example, you might invite Mr. Not-So-Bright or Mr. Garbage Head to your class.
2. Ask the character if he knows the memory verse. Of course, he will say no. Then ask him why not. He may reply, "Because I'm not so bright," or "Because my head is full of garbage."
3. Explain to the children the importance of learning memory verses. Remind them that they need to hide God's Word in their hearts.
4. Teach the memory verse to the character—and the children—by directing them to say the verse several times.

Memory Cheers

Materials:
1. Eight or 10 pom-poms
2. Four or five colorful baseball caps
3. Six to 10 sheets of poster board, depending on the length of the memory verse
4. Markers

Preparation:
1. From poster board, cut large cards approximately 12" x 18".
2. Cut as many cards as there are words in the memory verse.
3. Write the memory verse on the marker board.
4. Place the cards and markers at the back of the classroom.

Game Rules:
1. Select four or five children to be cheerleaders.
2. Have the cheerleaders go to the back of the classroom and create a cheer about the verse, using the pom-poms and cards. Each word of the verse may be written on a separate card.
3. Lead the children at their seats in a few songs, or practice saying the memory verse with them while the cheerleaders work.
4. After 5 to 10 minutes, have the cheerleaders come to the front of the classroom and present their cheer.
5. You may repeat this game by selecting four or five other children to create a cheer.

Alternative Idea:
1. To make this game competitive, divide the children into two teams: Team A and Team B (for example, a boys' team and a girls' team).
2. Challenge each team to create the best and loudest cheer.
3. Award prizes or points to the team with the best and loudest cheer.

26

Memory Puzzle

Materials:
1. Poster board
2. Straight edge
3. Two markers of different colors

Preparation:
1. On the sheet of poster board create a crossword puzzle that includes every word of the memory verse. Place numerals at the beginning of each word running horizontally or vertically.
2. Write in articles, conjunctions, and prepositions, or give the children clues such as "Word number one is a three-letter word that starts with *t* and ends with *e.*"
3. Design the crossword puzzle so it spells a key word or theme. The key word or theme is the mystery word. For example, if you use John 3:16, make a special rectangle with four letters in the middle of the puzzle for the word *love.*

Game Rules:
1. Divide the children into two teams: Team A and Team B (for example, a boys' team and a girls' team).
2. Tell the children that the puzzle contains the words of the memory verse.
3. Select a child from Team A to fill in one word of the puzzle.
4. Award a prize or team points if the child says the correct answer.
5. Select a child from Team B to fill in one word of the puzzle.
6. Award a prize or team points if the child says the correct answer.
7. Give bonus points to the child who solves the mystery word.
8. Continue playing until all the words have been filled in.
9. The team with the most points wins.

Memory Verse Songs

Materials:
1. Guitar, piano, or an audiotape of a scripture song you choose
2. Poster board
3. Marker

Preparation:
Write the memory verse on the sheet of poster board.

Game Rules:
1. Tell the children, "Today we are going to *sing* our memory verse."
2. Sing the song several times.
3. Encourage the children to sing with all their hearts.

Alternative Idea:
1. Divide the children into two teams: Team A and Team B (for example, a boys' team and a girls' team).
2. Challenge children of each team to sing their best.
3. Sing the song with each team.
4. Award points or prizes to the most expressive, most distinct, or loudest team of singers.

Missing Letters

Materials:

1. Poster board
2. Red and black markers

Preparation:

1. On the poster board make blanks that correspond to the letters of each word in the memory verse. For example, if the memory verse is Eph. 6:1—"Children, obey your parents"—the game board would look as follows: "_ _ _ _ _ _ _ _, _ _ _ _ _ _ _ _ _ _ _ _ _ _ _" (_ _ _ _ _ _ _ _ 6:1).
2. Lightly pencil in the letters for each blank to help administer the game faster and more smoothly.
3. Place the game board and the other marker at the front of the classroom.

Game Rules:

1. Divide the children into two teams: Team A and Team B (for example, a boys' team and a girls' team).
2. Tell the children they must guess the consonants first. Vowels are saved for the end if needed.
3. Choose a child from Team A to stand and guess one letter that is in the verse.
4. If the child guesses a letter that is in the verse, write the letter in the blank or blanks. Award the child team points for each blank filled in (for example, 50 points per consonant times the number of places the letter is found in the verse).
5. After all the blanks have been filled in, both teams say the memory verse. Remove the game board and have each team say the verse by memory.
6. The team with the most points wins.

Mystery Bust

Materials:
1. One balloon for each word in the memory verse
2. Thumbtacks
3. Bulletin board or sheet of plywood
4. Three throwing darts
5. Poster board
6. Paper, standard size
7. Marker
8. Masking tape

Preparation:
1. Cut the paper into fourths.
2. Write each word of the memory verse on a piece of paper.
3. Fold each piece of paper and place it inside a balloon.
4. Blow up the balloons.
5. Attach each balloon by the lip to the plywood or bulletin board with thumbtacks.
6. Place three or four tape lines about 6" apart on the floor in front of the game board to show children of different ages where to stand.

Game Rules:
1. Divide the children into two teams: Team A and Team B (for example, a boys' team and a girls' team).
2. Choose a child from Team A to come to the front of the classroom.
3. Give the child three darts, each one a chance to pop a balloon.
4. Award the child team points for each balloon popped.
5. Take the words from the popped balloons and place them onto the poster board in their respective positions.
6. Give the child an opportunity to say the memory verse.
7. Award the child prizes or points for saying the verse correctly.
8. Choose a child from Team B to come to the front of the classroom and proceed through steps 3 through 7.
9. Continue playing the game until all the balloons have been popped.
10. Have the children say the memory verse several times.
11. The team with the most points wins.

Puppet Pairs

Materials:
Two puppets dressed in contemporary clothes

Preparation:
1. Use the puppets to practice the dialogue below. Practice voice intonations and lip sync.
2. Name the puppets (for example, Lenny and Squiggy).

Dialogue:

LENNY and SQUIGGY: Teacher, teacher—we know the memory verse.

TEACHER: That's great. Tell the boys and girls the memory verse.

LENNY: Philippians 4:13.

SQUIGGY: "I

LENNY: can

SQUIGGY: do

LENNY: everything

SQUIGGY: through

LENNY: him

SQUIGGY: who

LENNY: gives

SQUIGGY: me

LENNY: strength."

SQUIGGY: Let's do it again, Lenny. This is fun. "I can do

LENNY: everything

SQUIGGY: through him who gives

LENNY: me strength."

LENNY and SQUIGGY: Yeah!

LENNY: You try it all by yourself, Squiggy.

SQUIGGY: All right. Philippians 4:13—"I can do everything through him who gives me strength."

LENNY and SQUIGGY: Yeah!

SQUIGGY: It's your turn, Lenny.

LENNY: Here I go. Philippians 4:13—"I can do everything through him who gives me strength."

LENNY and SQUIGGY: Yeah!

LENNY: Squiggy, let's see if the boys and girls can say the memory verse. Boys and girls, everyone say it together.

CHILDREN: Philippians 4:13—"I can do everything through him who gives me strength."

Lenny and Squiggy recite the Scripture verse several times, which helps the children learn their memory verse.

Puppeteer

Materials:
One hand puppet

Preparation:
1. Practice the dialogue below with the puppet.
2. Name the puppet (for example, "Bubba").

Dialogue:
TEACHER: Bubba, would you help the boys and girls learn our memory verse today?

BUBBA: Oh, sure. I'm really smart. I can teach these children their memory verse.

TEACHER: Good. Our memory verse today is 1 John 4:4—"The one who is in you is greater than the one who is in the world." Now you say it, Bubba.

BUBBA: OK. Uh, uh, uh—could you give me a hint?

TEACHER: Bubba, I thought you said you were smart.

BUBBA: Oh, I *am.* I just need a little hint.

TEACHER: Boys and girls, let's help Bubba. Everyone say the memory verse with me: 1 John 4:4.

CHILDREN: 1 John 4:4.

TEACHER: "The one who is in you is greater . . ."

CHILDREN: "The one who is in you is greater . . ."

TEACHER: "than the one who is in the world."

CHILDREN: "than the one who is in the world."

TEACHER: Bubba, try it again.

BUBBA: Here I go. 1 John 4:4. Uh, uh, uh—could you give me another hint? Just the first part!

TEACHER: All right. "The one"—

BUBBA: Yeah. That's right. "The one." Yeah, "the one." Uh, uh—1 John 4:4. "The one"—could you give me another hint?

TEACHER: Oh, Bubba. I know you're smarter than that. Boys and girls, let's help him again: 1 John 4:4.

CHILDREN: 1 John 4:4.

TEACHER: "The one who is in you is greater . . ."

CHILDREN: "The one who is in you is greater . . ."

TEACHER: "than the one who is in the world."

CHILDREN: "than the one who is in the world."

TEACHER: Bubba, try it again.

BUBBA: I've got it now, Teacher. It's, uh, 1 John 4:4. "The one who is"—uh, uh. Teacher, give me another hint. This is harder than I thought it was.

TEACHER: Boys and girls, repeat the memory verse one more time for Bubba. He needs to learn this verse. Here we go: 1 John 4:4.

CHILDREN: 1 John 4:4.

TEACHER: "The one who is in me is greater . . ."

CHILDREN: "The one who is in me is greater . . ."

TEACHER: "than the one who is in the world."

CHILDREN: "than the one who is in the world."

TEACHER: Bubba, now you try it.

The teacher and Bubba continue this dialogue until Bubba learns the memory verse. While Bubba is learning the verse, the children are learning it too.

Rip-off

Materials:
1. Paper, approximately 15' x 3'
2. Black wide-tipped marker

Preparation:
Write the memory verse on the long sheet of paper with big letters so the children can see the verse.

Game Rules:
1. Divide the children into two teams: Team A and Team B (for example, a boys' team and a girls' team).
2. Select six children to come to the front of the classroom to hold the paper.
3. Choose a child from Team A to stand and say the memory verse.
4. Award team points if the child says the verse correctly.
5. Rip off one word from the end of the memory verse.
6. Choose a child from Team B to stand and say the verse.
7. Award team points if the child says the verse correctly.
8. Rip off the next word from the end of the memory verse.
9. Continue playing the game until the verse has been completely ripped off and the children are saying the verse by memory.
10. The team with the most points wins.

Secret Code

Materials:

1. Two sheets of poster board
2. Two markers of different colors

Preparation:

1. Use one sheet of poster board on which to write a secret code, drawing a picture or simple symbol for each letter of the alphabet.
2. On the other sheet of poster board, write the memory verse by using the picture or symbols, leaving space between the lines so you can write the words of the memory verse above each coded word.

Game Rules:

1. Divide the children into two teams: Team A and Team B (for example, a boys' team and a girls' team).
2. Choose a child from Team A to come to the front of the classroom.
3. Have the child decode one word of the memory verse. As the child spells the word correctly, write it above the coded word.
4. Award the child team points according to the number of letters in the word. For example, a three-letter word is worth 300 points, a seven-letter word is worth 700 points, and so on.
5. Choose a child from Team B to come to the front of the classroom and proceed through steps 3 and 4.
6. Continue playing the game until the children have decoded the entire memory verse.
7. Have the teams recite the memory verse several times.
8. The team with the most points wins.

Sword Drill

Materials:
1. Bible for each child
2. Marker board
3. Marker for the marker board

Preparation:
Provide Bibles for children who do not bring their own.

Game Rules:
1. Pass out a Bible to each child who does not have one.
2. Tell the children to hold their Bibles over their heads.
3. Write a memory verse reference on the marker board.
4. On the count of three, children locate the Scripture reference.
5. The first child to find the reference, walk to the front of the class, and read the verse wins.
6. Award the winner a round of applause or a prize.
7. Play several rounds. You may even use the same Scripture reference more than once; however, do not allow the child who won the first time to read the same verse again.

Thy Word Is a Light

Materials:

1. Long sheet of paper, at least 3' by 10'
2. Black marker
3. Flashlight
4. Masking tape or thumb tacks

Preparation:

1. Print the memory verse across the long sheet of paper.
2. Right before time to play the game, attach paper to wall at front of the classroom or ask for two volunteers to hold each end of paper.
3. Turn off classroom lights.

Game Rules:

1. Use the flashlight to light up each word of memory verse as it is read.
2. Direct the class to read along as light is shone on each word.
3. Have the class read the verse several times.
4. Ask for volunteers to read the verse with light shining only on the Scripture reference. Teacher may choose to shine light on a different word as individual children read the verse.
5. Award prize or points to children who say the verse correctly.
6. Continue until most children have recited the verse correctly.

36

Tree of Life

Materials:
1. Large tree made from plywood, cardboard, or poster board
2. Poster board

Preparation:
1. Paint the tree with bright colors to attract the children's attention.
2. From the poster board cut fruit shapes (for example, apples, oranges, bananas). Cut a fruit shape for each word of the memory verse.
3. Hang the fruit on the tree so the children can read the memory verse.

Game Rules:
1. Divide the children into two teams: Team A and Team B (for example, a boys' team and a girls' team).
2. Choose a child from Team A to come to the front of the classroom.
3. Have the child read the memory verse.
4. Remove a piece of fruit from the tree, and tell the child to read the verse with the fruit missing.
5. Award a prize or team points if the child says the verse correctly.
6. Choose a child from Team B to come to the front of the classroom. Proceed through steps 3, 4, and 5.
7. Continue playing until all pieces of fruit have been removed from the tree.
8. The team with the most points wins.

Methods to Master Memory Verses

Bible Race

Materials:
Two "batons" (may be Bibles, banners, or decorated sticks)

Preparation:
1. Have batons ready.
2. Prepare a place for the children to walk for the relay, such as around the perimeters of the room or following footprints or arrows that lead through a designated course and then back to the starting point of the relay.

Game Rules:
1. Divide the children into two teams: Team A and Team B (for example, a boys' team and a girls' team).
2. Have the players come to the front of the classroom and line up in their teams.
3. On the count of three, each child at the front of the line recites the memory verse, takes the baton, walks through the designated course, and then hands the baton to the next child in line.
4. The first team to complete the relay wins.
5. Award prizes or points to the winning team.

Card Scramble

Materials:
1. Poster board
2. Markers

Preparation:
1. Use the poster board to cut cards approximately 4" x 10". Cut twice as many cards as there are words in the memory verse.
2. Write each word of the memory verse on a separate card.
3. Make a set of cards for each team.

Game Rules:
1. Divide the children into two teams: Team A and Team B (for example, a boys' team and a girls' team).
2. Choose a child from Team A and a child from Team B to come to the front of the classroom. The two children should be of similar age or ability.
3. Place a set of scrambled cards upside down in front of each child.
4. On the count of three, each child turns the cards over, unscrambles them, places the cards in correct order, and says the memory verse.
5. The first child to finish wins.
6. Award prizes or team points to the winner.
7. Continue playing for several rounds.
8. The team with the most points wins.

Children Scramble

Materials:
1. Poster board
2. Markers
3. Masking tape

Preparation:
1. Use the poster board to cut cards approximately 5" x 10". Cut twice as many cards as there are words in the memory verse.
2. Write each word of the memory verse on a separate card.
3. Make a set of cards for each team.

Game Rules:
1. Divide the children into two teams: Team A and Team B (for example, a boys' team and a girls' team).
2. Choose the same number of children from each team as there are words in the memory verse.
3. Line the children in teams facing the class.
4. Tape a card to the back of each child.
5. On the count of three, the children help their team members unscramble the memory verse and line up in the correct word order. Their backs need to face the class so the other children can read the verse.
6. The first team to unscramble and have a designated member say the memory verse wins.
7. Award prizes or points to the winning team.

Cookie Chew
or
Cracker Crunch

Materials:

1. Package of cookies or crackers
2. Two chairs
3. Chalkboard or poster board

Preparation:

1. Place two chairs at the front of the classroom about 15' apart, facing each other.
2. Write the memory verse on the chalkboard or poster board and set it at the front of the classroom.

Game Rules:

1. Divide the children into two teams: Team A and Team B (for example, a boys' team and a girls' team).
2. Select a child from Team A and a child from Team B to come to the front of the classroom and sit in the chairs that face each other.
3. Give each child a cookie or cracker.
4. On the count of three, each child eats a cookie or cracker, swallows it, and recites the memory verse.
5. The first child to eat a cookie or cracker, swallow it, and recite the verse wins.
6. Award the winner a prize or team points.
7. Select another child from Team A and Team B. Have the two children sit in the chairs and face each other. Proceed through steps 3, 4, 5, and 6.
8. Continue playing the game until all the cookies or crackers have been eaten.
9. The team with the most points wins.

44

Digging for Diamonds

Materials:
1. Twenty large plastic diamonds
2. One bucket
3. Two shovels

Preparation:
1. Hide the diamonds in the room before the children arrive.
2. Set the bucket and shovels at the front of the classroom.

Game Rules:
1. Divide the children into two teams: Team A and Team B (for example, a boys' team and a girls' team).
2. Choose a child from Team A and a child from Team B to come to the front of the classroom. The two children should be of similar age or ability.
3. On the count of three, direct the children to recite the memory verse as fast as possible and then run to "dig" a diamond. The children must use the shovels to dig and carry their diamonds. They cannot use their hands.
4. The first child to dig a diamond and put it into the bucket wins.
5. Award the winner team points.
6. Choose another child from each of the two teams to come to the front of the classroom. Proceed through steps 3, 4, and 5.
7. Continue playing the game until the children have dug all the diamonds.
8. The team with the most points wins.

Egg Hunt

Materials:

1. Twenty plastic eggs
2. One basket

Preparation:

1. Place points, treats, or bonus questions inside each egg.
2. Hide the eggs in the classroom before the children arrive.
3. Set the basket at the front of the classroom.

Game Rules:

1. Divide the children into two teams: Team A and Team B (for example, a boys' team and a girls' team).
2. Choose a child from Team A and a child from Team B to come to the front of the classroom. The two children should be of similar age or ability.
3. On the count of three, the children recite the memory verse as fast as possible. Then they run to hunt an egg.
4. The first child to place an egg into the basket wins.
5. Award the winner team points.
6. Choose another child from each of the two teams to come to the front of the classroom. Proceed through steps 3, 4, and 5.
7. Continue playing the game until the children have hunted all the eggs.
8. The team with the most points wins.

Flying Scriptures

Materials:
1. Ten Frisbees
2. Ten 3" x 5" index cards
3. Transparent tape
4. Black marker

Preparation:
1. Select five Scripture references of verses the children have learned.
2. Write each reference on two index cards.
3. Tape each card to the inside of a Frisbee.
4. Divide the Frisbees into two stacks. The Scripture verses need to be in the same order for each stack.
5. Set the two stacks of Frisbees at the front of the classroom.

Game Rules:
1. Divide the children into two teams: Team A and Team B (for example, a boys' team and a girls' team).
2. Direct each of the teams to sit in a separate area (for example, Team A sits on the left side of the classroom, Team B sits on the right side).
3. On the count of three, throw the first Frisbee of each stack. Throw one Frisbee to Team A and one to Team B. An assistant may be selected to help if the teacher cannot throw two Frisbees at the same time.
4. Team members are to catch the Frisbee, read the Scripture reference, and walk to the front of the classroom to recite the memory verse. Only one child from each team needs to recite the verse.
5. The first team to recite the verse is awarded a designated number of points.
6. Continue playing the game until all the Frisbees have been thrown.
7. The team with the most points wins.

Giant Killer

Materials:

1. Light-colored flannel material, approximately 84" x 45"
2. Three Ping-Pong balls
3. Velcro strips
4. Superglue or hot glue gun
5. Black marker

Preparation:

1. Use the marker to draw a giant on the flannel material, perhaps by using a transparency or opaque projector to trace it onto the material.
2. Divide the giant into point areas (for example, 200 points for the hands, 500 points for the heart, 1,000 points for the eyes, and so on).
3. Hang the giant onto a wall at the front of the classroom.
4. Glue narrow strips of Velcro to the Ping-Pong balls so that the hook side of the Velcro that adheres to flannel is exposed.

Game Rules:

1. Divide the children into two teams: Team A and Team B (for example, a boys' team and a girls' team).
2. Choose a child from Team A to come to the front of the classroom.
3. Give the child three Ping-Pong balls.
4. Direct the child to recite the memory verse before each throw. The child must recite the verse correctly to be allowed to throw a ball.
5. Award the appropriate number of team points for reciting the verse according to what point areas on the giant were hit.
6. Choose a child from Team B to come to the front of the classroom. Proceed through steps 3, 4, and 5.
7. Continue playing until each team member has had an opportunity to recite the memory verse.

Holy Hoops

Materials:
1. One small basketball hoop
2. One Nerf ball
3. Bulletin board

Preparation:
1. Mount the basketball hoop onto a bulletin board.
2. Set the Nerf ball at the front of the classroom near the basketball hoop.
3. Place three or four tape lines on the floor in front of the basketball hoop, designating where children of different ages should stand.

Game Rules:
1. Divide the children into two teams: Team A and Team B (for example, a boys' team and a girls' team).
2. Choose a child from Team A to come to the front of the classroom.
3. The child may shoot the ball three times. Direct the child to recite the memory verse each time before shooting the ball. The child must recite the verse correctly to be allowed to shoot the ball.
4. Award the child team points each time the ball goes through the hoop.
5. Select a child from Team B to come to the front of the classroom. Proceed through steps 3 and 4.
6. Continue playing the game until all team members have had an opportunity to say the memory verse.
7. The team with the most points wins.

49

Jailhouse

Materials:

1. Large picture of a thief or the devil
2. Black poster board
3. Transparent tape
4. Bulletin board

Preparation:

1. Attach the picture to the bulletin board.
2. Use the black poster board to make 1" strips for jail bars. Cut half as many jail bars as there are children in the class.
3. Attach pieces of tape to the backs of the jail bars so they are ready to hang over the picture.

Game Rules:

1. Explain to the children that "the thief comes only to steal and kill and destroy" (John 10:10), but it is a Christian's responsibility to put the thief behind bars by quoting Scripture verses.
2. Divide the children into two teams: Team A and Team B (for example, a boys' team and a girls' team).
3. Select a child from Team A and a child from Team B to come to the front of the classroom. The two children should be of similar age or ability.
4. On the count of three, direct the children to recite the memory verse as fast as they can.
5. The child who recites the memory verse the faster receives a jail bar to hang over the picture. The child is also awarded team points.
6. Choose another child from each of the two teams to come to the front of the classroom. Proceed through steps 4 and 5.
7. Continue playing until all the jail bars have been hung over the picture.
8. The team with the most points wins.

Last-Straw Holdup

Materials:
1. Twice as many straws as there are words in the memory verse
2. One-half the number of sheets of paper as there are words in the memory verse
3. Two markers of different colors

Preparation:
1. Place the straws at the front of the classroom.
2. Cut the paper into fourths. Use a colored marker to write each word of the memory verse on a separate piece of paper. Use the other marker to make a second set.
3. Spread all the pieces of paper onto the floor, right side up, at the back of the classroom so the children can see each word.

Game Rules:
1. Divide the children into two teams: Team A and Team B (for example, a boys' team and a girls' team). There must be the same number of children on each team as there are words in the memory verse.
2. Direct the children to come to the front of the classroom and line up in their teams.
3. Give each child a straw.
4. Explain to the team members which color of words they are to get.
5. Instruct that on the count of three they are to walk to the back of the classroom and use their straws to suck up one of the pieces of paper that has a memory verse word written on it in their team color.
6. They must carry their pieces of paper to the front of the classroom by continuing to suck through their straws. They cannot use their hands to hold the paper.
7. The children of each team must place their words in sequential order.
8. The first team to place the memory verse words in correct order and recite the verse wins.

Light My Path

Materials:
1. Two candles with handle guards
2. Matches or lighter

Preparation:
1. Place the candles and matches or lighter at the front of the classroom.
2. Designate a path you want the children to follow. The path may lead up and down an aisle or around the room. You may want to make arrows for the children to follow.

Game Rules:
1. Explain to the children that God's Word is like a light that shows them which path to follow in life.
2. Divide the children into two teams: Team A and Team B (for example, a boys' team and a girls' team).
3. Tell the children to come to the front of the classroom and line up in their teams.
4. Give the first child in each line a lighted candle with a handle guard.
5. On the count of three, the two children are to recite the memory verse, walk through the path, and hand the lighted candle to the next child in their team line.
6. The game continues until each child has said the memory verse and carried the candle through the path.
7. The first team to finish wins.
8. Award prizes to the winning team.

Alternative Idea:
1. Choose a child to come to the front of the classroom.
2. Give the child a lighted candle with a handle guard.
3. Direct the child to recite the memory verse as he or she walks through the path with the lighted candle. The child must say the verse loudly enough for the classmates to hear.
4. If the child says the verse correctly, award a round of applause or a prize.
5. Continue the game until every child has had a chance to say the verse and walk through the path.

52

Memory Dice

Materials:
Two large dice made from wood or foam

Preparation:
Place the dice at the front of the classroom.

Game Rules:
1. Divide the children into two teams: Team A and Team B (for example, a boys' team and a girls' team).
2. Choose a child from Team A and a child from Team B to come to the front of the classroom. The two children should be of similar age or ability.
3. Let each child roll a die.
4. On the count of three, the children say the memory verse as fast as they can.
5. The child who recites the verse the fastest receives the number of points he or she rolled on the die. The die points may be multiplied by 10 or 100. The other child does not receive any points.
6. Select another child from each of the two teams to come to the front of the classroom. Proceed through steps 3, 4, and 5.
7. Continue playing the game until every team member has had a turn.
8. The team with the most points wins.

Alternative Idea:
1. Choose a child to come to the front of the classroom.
2. Give the child a die to roll. The number on the rolled die determines the prize the child may win. (Before starting the game, the teacher designates prizes for each number on the die.)
3. Direct the child to recite the memory verse. Award the prize as determined by the die. For example, a 1 might allow the child to receive a sticker, a 3 a piece of sugarless candy, a 6 a poster, and so on.

Memory Match

Materials:

1. One 30" x 40" white foam board
2. Twenty-five 4" x 6" index cards
3. Twenty-five 3" x 5" index cards
4. Masking tape
5. Black marker

Preparation:

1. Number the 4" x 6" index cards from 1 to 25. Write the numerals almost as large as the cards.
2. Select 12 memory verses the children have learned.
3. Write the Scripture reference of each verse on two 3" x 5" index cards.
4. Select one more Scripture reference and write it on the remaining 3" x 5" card.
5. Scramble the 3" x 5" cards and place each one on the foam board an equal distance from each other so there are five horizontal rows and five vertical rows.
6. Tape the top edge of each card to the foam board.
7. Use the 4" x 6" cards to cover the 3" x 5" cards, placing them in sequential order from 1 to 25.
8. Tape the top edge of each 4" x 6" card to the foam board.

Game Rules:

1. Divide the children into two teams: Team A and Team B (for example, a boys' team and a girls' team).
2. Choose a child from Team A to select two numbers on the game board. If the Scripture references beneath the two numerals match, award Team A 1,000 points, and remove the two numeral cards and two Scripture reference cards. Direct the child to recite the memory verse of the reference. If the child correctly says the verse, award Team A an additional 2,000 points.
3. Choose a child from Team B to select two numbers on the game board. If the Scripture references beneath the two numerals match, award Team B 1,000 points, and remove the two numeral cards and two Scripture reference cards. If the child can correctly say the verse, award Team B an additional 2,000 points.
4. Continue playing until all the Scripture references have been matched.
5. The team with the most points wins.

Alternative Idea:

To make the game more challenging, remove the Scripture reference cards only when a child selects a match—but leave the top numeral cards attached.

Memory Mix-up

Materials:
1. Two sheets of poster board
2. Two markers of different colors

Preparation:
1. Write the words of the memory verse in random order on each of the two poster boards.
2. Set the two poster boards at the front of the classroom. Place a different-colored marker beside each poster board.

Game Rules:
1. Divide the children into two teams: Team A and Team B (for example, a boys' team and a girls' team).
2. Choose the same number of children from each team as there are words in the memory verse.
3. Line the children up beside their team's poster board.
4. On the count of three, the first child in each line walks to the team poster board, circles the first word in the verse, and draws a line to the second word in the verse. Then the child walks back and tags the next child in line.
5. The second child in line walks to the poster board, circles the second word in the verse, and draws a line to the third word. Then the child walks back and tags the next child in line.
6. After the last child in line completes a turn, all the team members recite the memory verse.
7. The first team to recite the verse wins.
8. Award prizes to the winning team.

Mining for Gold

Materials:
1. Twenty rocks painted gold
2. One bucket
3. Two plastic sand shovels

Preparation:
1. Hide the gold nuggets in the classroom before the children arrive.
2. Place the bucket and shovels at the front of the classroom.

Game Rules:
1. Divide the children into two teams: Team A and Team B (for example, a boys' team and a girls' team).
2. Select a child from Team A and a child from Team B to come to the front of the classroom. The two children should be of similar age or ability.
3. On the count of three, the children recite the memory verse as fast as they can. Then they walk to "mine" a gold nugget. The children must use their shovels to mine the gold and carry it to the bucket at the front of the classroom. They cannot mine or carry the gold with their hands.
4. The first child to place a gold nugget into the bucket wins.
5. Award the winner team points.
6. Select another child from each of the two teams to come to the front of the classroom. Proceed through steps 3, 4, and 5.
7. Continue playing the game until the children have mined all the gold nuggets.
8. The team with the most points wins.

Path of Righteousness

Materials:
1. Construction paper
2. Grand prize

Preparation:
1. Use the construction paper to cut footprints. A child's tennis shoe makes a good pattern. Make twice as many footprints as there are children in your class.
2. Establish a starting point for Team A and a starting point for Team B. The two starting points need to be of equal distance from the grand prize, yet different from the place where the two teams line up.

Game Rules:
1. Divide the children into two teams: Team A and Team B (for example, a boys' team and a girls' team).
2. Instruct the children to come to the front of the classroom and line up in their teams.
3. Give each child a footprint.
4. On the count of three, the first child in each line walks to the team's starting point and recites the memory verse as fast as possible. Then the child places a footprint from the starting point going toward the grand prize. The child walks back and tags the next team member in line.
5. The next child walks to the starting point and recites the memory verse as fast as possible. Then the child places a footprint next to the toe of the last footprint. The child walks back and tags the next team member in line.
6. This process continues until one of the teams reaches the grand prize. The first team to reach the grand prize wins. The grand prize may be a bucket of peanuts or candy for the team.

57

Pearl of Great Price

Materials:
1. 20 Ping-Pong balls
2. Small chest or shoe box
3. Gold spray paint

Preparation:
1. Paint the chest or box gold to create a treasure chest.
2. Place the treasure chest at the front of the classroom.
3. Hide the "pearls," or Ping-Pong balls, in the classroom before the children arrive.

Game Rules:
1. Divide the children into two teams: Team A and Team B (for example, a boys' team and a girls' team).
2. Select a child from Team A and a child from Team B to come to the front of the classroom. The two children should be of similar age or ability.
3. On the count of three, the children recite the memory verse as fast as possible and then run to find a pearl.
4. The first child to place a pearl into the treasure chest wins.
5. Award the winner team points.
6. Choose another child from each of the two teams to come to the front of the classroom. Proceed through steps 3, 4, and 5.
7. Continue playing the game until the children have found all the pearls.
8. The team with the most points wins.

58

Pocket Scramble

Materials:
1. Two pocket charts
2. Poster board
3. Marker

Preparation:
1. Use the poster board to cut cards approximately 3" x 5". Cut twice as many cards as there are words in the memory verse.
2. Write each word of the memory verse on a card.
3. Make a set of cards for each team.
4. Set the pocket charts at the front of the classroom.
5. Place a set of scrambled cards next to each pocket chart.

Game Rules:
1. Divide the children into two teams: Team A and Team B (for example, a boys' team and a girls' team).
2. Select a child from Team A and a child from Team B to come to the front of the classroom. The two children should be of similar age or ability.
3. On the count of three, direct the children to unscramble the memory verse cards, place them in correct order into the pockets, and say the memory verse.
4. The first child to finish wins.
5. Award the winner a prize or team points.
6. Choose another child from each of the two teams to come to the front of the classroom. Proceed through steps 3, 4, and 5.
7. Continue playing the game for several rounds.
8. The team with the most points wins.

59

Pyramid Climb

Materials:
1. Poster board
2. Two tokens

Preparation:
1. Draw a pyramid on the poster board. The pyramid should have at least five steps on each side that lead to the top.
2. Place each token on a bottom step of the pyramid.

Game Rules:
1. Divide the children into two teams: Team A and Team B (for example, a boys' team and a girls' team).
2. Choose a child from Team A and a child from Team B to come to the front of the classroom. The two children should be of similar age or ability.
3. On the count of three, the children recite the memory verse as fast as they can.
4. The first child to recite the verse wins and moves his or her team's token one step up the pyramid.
5. Choose another child from each of the two teams to come to the front of the classroom. Proceed through steps 3 and 4.
6. Continue playing until one team reaches the top of the pyramid.
7. The first team to reach the top wins.
8. Award prizes to the winning team.

Rapid Fire

Materials:
1. Eighty to 100 small balloons
2. Two bulletin boards, approximately 5' x 5'
3. Thumbtacks
4. Ten throwing darts
5. Masking tape

Preparation:
1. Inflate the balloons.
2. Attach half of the balloons by their lips with thumbtacks to one bulletin board and the other half to the other bulletin board.
3. Place the boards about 10' apart.
4. Place three or four tape lines about 6" apart on the floor, designating the distance for players of different ages.

Game Rules:
1. Divide the children into two teams: Team A and Team B (for example, a boys' team and a girls' team).
2. Select a child from Team A and a child from Team B to come to the front of the classroom. The two children should be of similar age or ability.
3. Each child stands in front of his or her team bulletin board.
4. Give each child five throwing darts.
5. On the count of three, each child recites the memory verse as fast as possible and then throws a dart. The children must recite the memory verse each time before throwing a dart.
6. The two children continue to recite the verse and throw their darts until they have thrown all their darts.
7. Award prizes or team points for each balloon popped. Award bonus points to the child who finishes first.
8. Choose another child from each of the two teams to come to the front of the classroom. Proceed through steps 3, 4, 5, 6, and 7.
9. Continue playing for several rounds or until all the balloons have been popped.
10. The team with the most points wins.

Alternative Idea:
1. Choose a child to stand in front of the bulletin board.
2. Give the child five throwing darts.
3. Direct the child to recite the memory verse each time before throwing a dart.
4. Award prizes according to the number of balloons popped.

61

Scripture Scramble

Materials:
1. Two Velcro boards (or two boards covered with flannel material)
2. Velcro strips
3. Transparencies
4. Poster board
5. Transparency markers

Preparation:
1. From the poster board, cut cards approximately 3" x 5". Cut twice as many cards as there are words in the memory verse.
2. From the transparencies, cut rectangles, approximately 3" x 5". Cut twice as many pieces as there are words in the memory verse.
3. Glue or tape a piece of transparency to the front of each card.
4. Attach a Velcro strip to the back of each card so it will adhere to the Velcro or flannel board.
5. Use a transparency marker to write each word of the memory verse on a card. This allows the cards to be wiped clean and used again.
6. Make a set of cards for each team.
7. Place a set of scrambled cards next to each Velcro or flannel board.

Game Rules:
1. Divide the children into two teams: Team A and Team B (for example, a boys' team and a girls' team).
2. Select a child from Team A and a child from Team B to come to the front of the classroom. The two children should be of similar age or ability.
3. Give each child a set of scrambled cards.
4. On the count of three, direct the children to unscramble the memory verse cards, place them in correct order on the Velcro board, and recite the verse.
5. The first child to unscramble and recite the verse correctly wins.
6. Award the winner a prize or team points.
7. Choose another child from each of the two teams to come to the front of the classroom. Proceed through steps 3, 4, 5, and 6.
8. Continue playing for several rounds.
9. The team with the most points wins.

Alternative Idea:
Use magnetic boards and magnetic strips.

Swords

Materials:
1. Poster board
2. Black marker
3. Cardboard or wood
4. Silver spray paint

Preparation:
1. Write the memory verse on the poster board.
2. Use the cardboard or wood to cut swords.
3. Paint the swords silver.

Game Rules:
1. Divide the children into two teams: Team A and Team B (for example, a boys' team and a girls' team).
2. Select a child from Team A and a child from Team B to come to the front of the classroom. The two children should be of similar age or ability.
3. Lay a sword on the floor next to each child.
4. On the count of three, direct the children to take three steps, turn and face each other, recite the memory verse as fast as possible, pick up a sword, and raise it into the air.
5. The first child to raise a sword wins.
6. Award the winner a prize or team points.
7. Choose another child from each of the two teams to come to the front of the classroom. Proceed through steps 4, 5, and 6.
8. Continue playing the game for several rounds or until all the children have had a turn to recite the memory verse.
9. The team with the most points wins.

Three in a Row

Materials:

1. One large sheet of poster board
2. Transparencies (enough to make nine 4" x 6" rectangles)
3. Nine 3" x 5" white index cards
4. Nine 3" x 5" colored index cards
5. Nine 4" x 6" white index cards
6. Colored tape
7. Glue
8. Black marker
9. Black transparency marker

Preparation:

1. Cut the transparencies into nine 4" x 6" rectangles.
2. Cover each 4" x 6" card with a transparency rectangle.
3. Place the 4" x 6" index cards equal distances from each other so there are three horizontal rows and three vertical rows.
4. Tape the left, right, and bottom sides of each 4" x 6" card to the poster board to make nine pockets.
5. Label the corner of each card with one of the following: TL (top left), TC (top center), TR (top right), CL (center left), C (center), CR (center right), BL (bottom left), BC (bottom center), BR (bottom right).
6. Write a different Scripture verse on each of the white 3" x 5" index cards. Write the same nine Scripture verses on the colored 3" x 5" index cards, one verse per card.
7. Place a white 3" x 5" index card and a colored 3" x 5" index card in each of the nine pockets on the board. The same Scripture verses do not have to be in each pocket.
8. Place the game board at the front of the classroom.

Game Rules:

1. Tell the children that they are going to play a memory verse review game that is similar to ticktacktoe. They must get their team symbol onto three pockets in a row.
2. Divide the children into two teams: Team A and Team B (for example, a boys' team and a girls' team).
3. Assign the two teams white or colored cards, and give each a symbol. Be creative. Don't use simply X's and O's.
4. Choose a child from Team A to come to the front of the classroom.
5. Direct the child to select one of the pockets: TL, TC, TR, CL, C, CR, BL, BC, or BR.
6. Pull out the appropriate card in the pocket for that team. Read

the Scripture verse aloud. If the child recites the memory verse correctly, write the team symbol on the pocket. If the child fails to recite the verse correctly, place the card back into the pocket and leave the pocket blank.

7. Choose a child from Team B to come to the front of the classroom. Proceed through steps 3 and 4.

8. Continue playing until one team gets their symbol written on three pockets in a row.

Alternative Idea:

The teacher decides whether to allow more than one team's symbol on a pocket. By allowing more than one symbol, one of the two teams always wins. Otherwise, some games result in no team winning.

65

Wild Whistle

Materials:

1. Whistle
2. Poster board
3. Black marker
4. Cloth to cover the poster board

Preparation:

1. Write the reference of the memory verse on the poster board large enough so all the children can see it.
2. Cover the poster board.

Game Rules:

1. During the lesson or service, periodically and without warning, blow the whistle.
2. At the sound of the whistle, uncover the poster board with the memory verse reference written on it.
3. The first child to raise his or her hand recites the memory verse.
4. Award a prize to the first child who is able to recite the verse correctly.